The Book Of Arda Viraf: A Dantesque Vision Of Heaven And Hell

Charles F. Horne

Kessinger Publishing's Rare Reprints

Thousands of Scarce and Hard-to-Find Books
on These and other Subjects!

- Americana
- Ancient Mysteries
- Animals
- Anthropology
- Architecture
- Arts
- Astrology
- Bibliographies
- Biographies & Memoirs
- Body, Mind & Spirit
- Business & Investing
- Children & Young Adult
- Collectibles
- Comparative Religions
- Crafts & Hobbies
- Earth Sciences
- Education
- Ephemera
- Fiction
- Folklore
- Geography
- Health & Diet
- History
- Hobbies & Leisure
- Humor
- Illustrated Books
- Language & Culture
- Law
- Life Sciences

- Literature
- Medicine & Pharmacy
- Metaphysical
- Music
- Mystery & Crime
- Mythology
- Natural History
- Outdoor & Nature
- Philosophy
- Poetry
- Political Science
- Science
- Psychiatry & Psychology
- Reference
- Religion & Spiritualism
- Rhetoric
- Sacred Books
- Science Fiction
- Science & Technology
- Self-Help
- Social Sciences
- Symbolism
- Theatre & Drama
- Theology
- Travel & Explorations
- War & Military
- Women
- Yoga
- *Plus Much More!*

We kindly invite you to view our catalog list at:
http://www.kessinger.net

THE BOOK OF ARDA VIRAF

CHAPTER I [1]

IN THE NAME OF GOD [2]

1. They say that, once upon a time, the pious Zaratusht [3] made the religion, which he had received, current in the world;

2. and till the completion of 300 years, the religion was in purity, and men were without doubts.

3. But afterward, the accursed evil spirit, the wicked one, in order to make men doubtful of this religion,

4. instigated the accursed Alexander, the Roman,[4]

5. who was dwelling in Egypt, so that he came to the country of Iran,

6. and destroyed the metropolis and empire, and made them desolate.

7. And this religion,[5] namely, all the Avesta and Zend, written upon prepared cow-skins, and with gold ink, was deposited in the archives, in Stakhar Papakan,[6]

8. and the hostility of the evil-destined, wicked Ashemok, the evil-doer, brought onward Alexander, the Roman, who was dwelling in Egypt, and he burned them up.[7]

[1] Translated by Prof. Martin Haug, of the University of Munich.

[2] Prof. Haug translated, or rather revised, this work from the MS. of a Parsi priest Hoshangji.

[3] Zoroaster.

[4] That is, a native of those Greek provinces which afterward became an important part of the eastern empire of the Romans.

[5] That is, the religious writings.

[6] The name of Persepolis in Sassanian times.

[7] This statement, regarding the burning of the religious books by Alexander, which often occurs in Parsi writings, has been supposed to have originated in a modern misunderstanding, whereby the destruction consequent upon the Mohammedan conquest has been attributed to the Greek invader. Heeren first expressed the opinion that, as the persecution of foreign religions was quite contrary to Alexander's policy, this

9. And he killed several *Desturs* and judges and *Herbads* and *Mobads* and upholders of the religion,[8] and the competent and wise of the country of Iran.

10. And he cast hatred and strife, one with the other, amongst the nobles and householders of the country of Iran;

11. and self-destroyed, he fled to hell.[9]

12. And after that, there were confusion and contention among the people of the country of Iran, one with the other.

13. And so they had no lord, nor ruler, nor chieftain, nor *Destur* who was acquainted with the religion,

14. and they were doubtful in regard to God;

15. and religions of many kinds, and different fashions of belief, and skepticism, and various codes of law were promulgated in the world;

16. until the time when the blessed and immortal Ataropad-i Marspendan was born; on whose breast, in the tale which is in the Din-kard,[10] melted brass was poured.

17. And much law and justice were administered according to different religions and different creeds;

18. and the people of this religion[11] deposited in Shaspigan[12] were in doubt.

19. And afterward, there were other magi and *Desturs* of the religion;

statement of the Parsis was not to be credited; and his opinion has been generally adopted by later writers, without further examination. On comparing, however, the statements made in Pahlavi books with the accounts of the destruction of Persepolis, given by classical writers, it appears that the latter rather confirm, than contradict, the statements of the Parsis.

[8] These names refer to the various grades of the Zoroastrian priesthood.

[9] This appears to refer to Alexander's premature death.

[10] The words *dino-karto* can only refer to that large and comprehensive collection of old religious traditions, which goes by the name of " Din-kard," and was compiled from a far more extensive Zend and Pahlavi literature than that which has reached our time.

[11] Religious books.

[12] That is, those who believed in the religious writings deposited in the treasure of Shaspigan.

20. and some of their number were loyal and apprehensive.

21. And an assembly of them was summoned in the residence of the victorious Frobag fire; [13]

22. and there were speeches and good ideas, of many kinds, on this subject:

23. that " it is necessary for us to seek a means,

24. so that some one of us may go, and bring intelligence from the spirits;

25. that the people who exist in this age shall know

26. whether these Yazishn and Dron and Afrinagan ceremonies, and Nirang prayers, and ablution and purifications [14] which we bring into operation, attain unto God, or unto the demons;

27. and come to the relief of our souls, or not."

28. Afterward also, with the concurrence of the *Desturs* of the religion, they called all the people to the residence of the Frobag fire.

29. And from the whole number they set apart seven men who had not the slightest doubt of God and the religion,

30. and whose own thoughts and words and deeds were most orderly and proper;

31. and they were told thus: " Seat yourselves down,

32. and select one from among you, who is best for this duty, and the most innocent and respected."

33. And afterward, those seven men sat down;

34. and, from the seven, three were selected; and from the three, one only, named Viraf;

35. and some call him the Nishapurian.

36. Then that Viraf, as he heard that decision, stood upon his feet,

37. joined his hands on his breast, and spoke

[13] This is one of the three most ancient fires in Iran, which were held in great reverence, and are mentioned in various Pahlavi books.

[14] These ceremonies, which are all accompanied by prayers, are commonly practised by Parsi priests at the present day.

38. thus: "If it please you, then give me not the undesired narcotic [15]

39. till you cast lots for the Mazdayasnians and me;

40. and if the lot come to me, I shall go willingly to that place of the pious and the wicked,

41. and carry this message correctly, and bring an answer truly."

42. And afterward, the lots of those Mazdayasnians and me were drawn;

43. the first time with the word "well-thought," and the second time with the word "well-said," and the third time with the word "well-done"; each of the three lots came to Viraf.

CHAPTER II

1. And that Viraf had seven sisters,

2. and all those seven sisters were as wives [1] of Viraf;

3. they had also learned the religion of heart, and recited the prayers.

4. And when they heard those tidings, then they came upon them so very grievously,

5. that they clamored and shrieked,

[15] When natives of India wish to obtain supernatural information they sometimes give, it is said, a narcotic prepared from the seeds of the *dhattura* plant, to a boy or old man, and place much reliance upon his answers to their questions, while under its intoxicating influence.

[1] This incident appears to be introduced merely as an illustration of the extraordinary piety of Viraf, in obeying the precepts of his religion with regard to Khvaetvadatha, or "next-of-kin marriage"; it also indicates that the tale was written before the ancient practise of marriage between brothers and sisters was discontinued. The later Pazand and Persian MSS. obscure the meaning by omitting this sentence; and, by sometimes changing "sisters" into "wives," and "brother" into "husband," conveys the idea that Viraf had seven wives who were merely sisters to each other. Destur Hoshangji thinks that they were not married, but only a sisterhood of nuns, in imitation of Christian customs; though he admits that there is no evidence that such an institution ever existed among Zoroastrians. If, however, they were married, he thinks it may have been merely a nominal marriage. As an instance of the ancient practise of marriage between brother and sister may be mentioned that of Cambyses, son of Cyrus, with his sister Atossa.

6. and went into the presence of the assembly of the Mazdayasnians,

7. and they stood up and bowed,

8. and said thus: "Do not this things, ye Mazdayasnians;

9. for we are seven sisters, and he is an only brother;

10. and we are, all seven sisters, as wives of that brother.

11. Just as the door of a house, in which seven lintels [2] were fixed, and one post below,

12. they who shall take away that post will make those lintels fall;

13. so for us seven sisters is this only brother, who is our life and maintenance;

14. every benefit from him proceeds from God.

15. Should you send him, before his time, from this realm of the living to that of the dead,

16. you will commit an injustice on us without cause."

17. And afterward, those Mazdayasnians, when they heard those words, pacified those seven sisters,

18. and said thus: "We will deliver Viraf to you, safe and sound,[3] in seven days;

19. and the happiness of this renown will remain with this man."

20. Then they became satisfied.

21. And then Viraf joined his hands on his breast before the Mazdayasnians, and said to them

22. thus: "It is the custom that I should pray to the departed souls, and eat food, and make a will; afterward, you will give me the wine and narcotic."

23. The *Desturs* directed thus: "Act accordingly."[4]

24. And afterward, those *Desturs* of the religion selected,

2 Or "joists"; the meaning may be that the lintel of the doorway was formed of seven narrow timbers laid, side by side, over the opening, which, when large timber is scarce and walls are thick, is an easy way of making a large lintel; or it may refer to an entrance-verandah, in which one post supports seven joists by means of a post-plate.

3 Literally, "healthy."

4 That is, in accordance with the custom mentioned by Viraf.

in the dwelling of the spirit,[5] a place which was thirty footsteps from the good.[6]

25. And Viraf washed his head and body, and put on new clothes;

26. he fumigated himself with sweet scent [7] and spread a carpet, new and clean, on a prepared couch.

27. He sat down on the clean carpet of the couch,

28. and consecrated the Dron, and remembered the departed souls, and ate food.

29. And then those *Desturs* of the religion filled three golden cups with wine and narcotic of Vishtasp;

30. and they gave one cup over to Viraf with the word " well-thought," and the second cup with the word " well-said," and the third cup with the word " well-done ";

31. and he swallowed the wine and narcotic, and said grace whilst conscious, and slept upon the carpet.

32. Those *Desturs* of the religion and the seven sisters were occupied, seven days and nights, with the ever-burning fire and fumigations; and they recited the Avesta and Zend of the religious ritual,

33. and recapitulated the Nasks,[8] and chanted the Gathas,[9] and kept watch in the dark.

34. And those seven sisters sat around the carpet of Viraf,

35. and seven days and nights the Avesta was repeated.

36. Those seven sisters with all the *Desturs* and *Herbads*

[5] That is, the dwelling of the angel of fire, Ataro yedato, the fire-temple in which they were assembled, previously called " the residence of the Frobag fire."

[6] Literally, " as to that which is good." As the soul of Viraf was about to quit the body, it was necessary that the latter should be treated as a dead body, and be kept thirty footsteps away from fire, water, and other holy things.

[7] Such fumigation is not now practised by the Parsis.

[8] The Nasks, or " books," of the Avesta are frequently mentioned in the Parsi writings. They comprised the whole religious and scientific literature of the Zoroastrian priesthood. It is doubtful whether the recapitulation of the Nasks refers to the whole of them, or only a portion; but it means, probably, only a recital of their general contents, as it can scarcely be supposed that all the Nasks were extant, in their entirety, in the time of Arda Viraf.

[9] The recital of the five Gathas is compulsory on every Zoroastrian.

and *Mobads* of the religion of the Mazdayasnians, discontinued not their protection in any manner.

CHAPTER III

1. And the soul of Viraf went, from the body, to the Kinvat bridge of Chakat-i-Daitik,

2. and came back the seventh day,[1] and went into the body.

3. Viraf rose up, as if he arose from a pleasant sleep,

4. thinking of Vohuman[2] and joyful.

5. And those sisters, with the *Desturs* of the religion and the Mazdayasnians, when they saw Viraf, became pleased and joyful;

6. and they said thus: " Be thou welcome, Viraf, the messenger of us Mazdayasnians, who art come from the realm of the dead to this realm of the living.

7. Those *Herbads* and *Desturs* of the religion bowed before Viraf.

8. And then Viraf, as he saw them, came forward and bowed, and said thus: " For you is a blessing from Auharmazd, the lord, and the archangels (Amshaspands);

9. and a blessing from the pious Zaratusht, the descendant of Spitama;

10. and a blessing from Srosh the pious, and Ataro the angel (*Yazad*), and the glorious religion of the Mazdayasnians;

11. and a blessing from the remaining pious; and a blessing from the remaining spirits of paradise who are in happiness and repose."

12. And afterward, the *Desturs* of the religion said

13. thus: " A faithful minister[3] art thou, Viraf, who art the messenger of us Mazdayasnians; and may thy blessing be for thee also.

---

[1] Literally, " day and night "; that is, the natural day of twenty-four hours.

[2] That is, " inspired with good thoughts."

[3] Literally, " a proper servant."

14. Whatever thou sawest, relate to us truly."

15. Then Viraf spoke thus: "First this is to be said,

16. that to give the hungry and thirsty food is the first thing,

17. and afterward to make inquiry of him, and appoint his task."

18. Then the *Desturs* of the religion assented[4] thus: "Well and good."

19. And well-cooked and savory[5] food and broth, and cold water and wine were brought.

20. They also consecrated the ceremonial cake (*dron*); and Viraf muttered grace, and ate the food, and having finished the sacred repast (*myazd*), he said grace.

21. And he recounted the praises of Auharmazd and the archangels; and he muttered the benedictions (*afrinagan*).

22. He also directed thus: "Bring a writer who is wise and learned."

23. And an accomplished writer, who was learned, was brought by him, and sat before him;

24. and whatsoever Viraf said, he wrote correctly, clearly, and explicitly.

CHAPTER IV

1. And he ordered him to write

2. thus: In that first night, Srosh the pious and Ataro the angel came to meet me,

3. and they bowed to me, and spoke

4. thus: "Be thou welcome, Arda Viraf, although thou hast come when it is not thy time."[1]

5. I said: "I am a messenger."

6. And then the victorious Srosh the pious, and Ataro the angel, took hold of my hand.

---

[4] Literally, " ordered."
[5] Literally, " well-scented."
[1] Although the time of thy coming is not yet.

7. Taking the first footstep with the good thought, and the second footstep with the good word, and the third footstep with the good deed, I came up to the Chinvat [2] bridge, the very wide [3] and strong and created by Auharmazd.

8. When I came up there,

9. I saw a soul of the departed, whilst in those first three nights the soul was seated on the top of the body.

10. and uttered those words of the Gatha:

11. *" Ushta ahmai yahmai ushta kahmaichid ";* that is, " Well is he by whom that which is his benefit becomes the benefit of any one else."

12. And in those three nights, as much benefit and comfort and enjoyment came to it,

13. as all the benefit which it beheld in the world;

14. just as a man who, whilst he was in the world, was more comfortable and happy and joyful through it.

15. In the third dawn, that soul of the pious departed into the sweet scent of trees;

16. and he considered that scent which passed by his nose among the living;

17. and the air of that fragrance comes from the more southern side, from the direction of God.

18. And there stood before him his own religion and his own deeds, in the graceful form of a damsel, as a beautiful appearance, that is, grown up in virtue;

19. with prominent breasts, that is, her breasts swelled downward, which is charming to the heart and soul;

20. whose form was as brilliant, as the sight of it was the more well-pleasing, the observation of it more desirable.

21. And the soul of the pious asked that damsel

22. thus: " Who art thou? and what person art thou? than whom, in the world of the living, any damsel more elegant, and of more beautiful body than thine, was never seen by me."

[2] Or Kinvat.
[3] " The refuge of many."

23. To him replied she who was his own religion and his own deeds,

24. thus: "I am thy actions, O youth of good thoughts, of good words, of good deeds, of good religion.

25. It is on account of thy will and actions that I am as great and good and sweet-scented and triumphant and undistressed as appears to thee.

26. For in the world the Gathas were chanted by thee, and the good water was consecrated by thee, and the fire tended by thee;

27. and the pious man who came from far, and who was from near, was honored by thee.

28. Though I have been stout, I am made stouter through thee;

29. and though I have been virtuous, I am made more virtuous through thee;

30, 31. and though I have been seated on a resplendent throne, I am seated more resplendently through thee;

32. and though I have been exalted, I am made more exalted through thee;

33. through these good thoughts and good words and good deeds which thou practisedst.

34. They honored thee, and the pious man after thee,

35. in that long worship and communion with Auharmazd, when thou performedst, for Auharmazd, worship and proper conversation for a long time.

36. Peace be from it."

CHAPTER V

1. Afterward, the width of that Chinvat bridge became again nine javelin-lengths.

2. With the assistance of Srosh the pious, and Ataro the angel, I passed over easily, happily, courageously, and triumphantly, on the Chinvat bridge.

3, 4. I had much protection from Mitro the angel, and Rashn the just, and Vai the good, and the angel Vahram the powerful, and the angel Ashtad the world-increasing, and the glory of the good religion of the Mazdayasnians; and the guardian angels [1] of the pious, and the remaining spirits first bowed to me, Arda Viraf.

5. I also saw, I Arada Viraf, Rashn the just, who held in his hand the yellow golden balance, and weighed the pious and the wicked.

6. And afterward, Srosh the pious, and Ataro the angel, took hold of my hand,

7. and said thus: " Come on, so that we may show unto thee heaven and hell; and the splendor and glory and ease and comfort and pleasure and joy and delight and gladness and fragrance which are the reward of the pious in heaven.

8. We shall show thee the darkness and confinement and ingloriousness and misfortune and distress and evil and pain and sickness and dreadfulness and fearfulness and hurtfulness and stench in the punishments of hell, of various kinds, which the demons and sorcerers and sinners perform.

9. We shall show thee the place of the true and that of the false.

10. We shall show thee the reward of the firm believers in Auharmazd and the archangels, and the good which is in heaven, and the evil which is in hell;

11. and the reality of God and the archangels, and the non-reality of Akharman and the demons; and the existence of the resurrection of the dead and the future body.

12. We shall show thee the reward of the pious, from Auharmazd and the archangels, in the midst of heaven.

13. We shall show thee the torment and punishment of various kinds, which are for the wicked, in the midst of hell, from Akharman and the molestations of the demons."

CHAPTER VI

1. I came to a place,

2. and I saw the souls of several people, who remain in the same position.

3. And I asked the victorious Srosh the pious, and Ataro

---

[1] Every creature and object created by Auharmazd is supposed to possess a spiritual representative in the other world.

the angel, thus: "Who are they? and why remain they here?"

4. Srosh the pious, and Ataro the angel, said

5. thus: "They call this place *Hamestagan;* [1]

6. and these souls remain in this place till the future body; [2]

7. and they are the souls of those men whose good works and sin were equal.

8. Speak out to the worlds thus: 'Let not avarice and vexation prevent you from doing a very easy good work, [3]

9. for every one whose good works are three *Srosho-charanam* more than his sin goes to heaven.

10. they whose sin is more go to hell;

11. they in whom both are equal remain among these Hamestagan till the future body.'

12. Their punishment is cold, or heat, from the revolution of the atmosphere; and they have no other adversity."

CHAPTER VII

1. And afterward, I put forth the first footstep to the star track, on Humat, the place where good thoughts (*humat*) are received with hospitality.

2. And I saw those souls of the pious whose radiance, which ever increased, was glittering as the stars;

3. and their throne and seat were under the radiance, and splendid and full of glory.

4. And I asked Srosh the pious, and Ataro the angel, thus: "Which place is this? and which people are these?"

5. Srosh the pious, and Ataro the angel, said

6. thus: "This place is the star tract; and those are the souls

7. who, in the world, offered no prayers, and chanted no Gathas, and contracted no next-of-kin marriage;

[1] The ever-stationary. .
[2] That is, "the resurrection."
[3] Consider not the easier good works with avarice and as vexation.

8. they have also exercised no sovereignty, nor rulership nor chieftainship.

9. Through other good works they have become pious."

CHAPTER VIII

1. When I put forth the second footstep, it was to Hukht of the moon track, the place where good words (*hukht*) find hospitality;

2. and I saw a great assembly of the pious.

3. And I asked Srosh the pious, and Ataro the angel, thus: " Which place is this? and who are those souls? "

4. Srosh the pious, and Ataro the angel, said

5. thus: " This place is the moon track; and these are those souls who, in the world, offered no prayers, and chanted no Gathas, and contracted no next-of-kin marriages;

6. but through other good works they have come hither;

7. and their brightness is like unto the brightness of the moon."

CHAPTER IX

1. When I put forth the third footstep on Huvarsht, there where good deeds (*huvarsht*) are received with hospitality, there I arrived.

2. There is the radiance which they call the highest of the highest;

3. and I saw the pious on thrones and carpets made of gold;

4. and they were people whose brightness was like unto the brightness of the sun.

5. And I asked Srosh the pious, and Ataro the angel, thus: " Which place is this? and who are those souls? "

6. Srosh the pious, and Ataro the angel, said

7. thus: " This is the sun track; and those are the souls who, in the world, exercised good sovereignty and rulership and chieftainship."

CHAPTER X

1. I put forth the fourth footstep unto the radiance of Garodman, the all-glorious;

2. and the souls of the departed came to meet us, and they asked a blessing, and offered praise,

3. and they spoke thus: "How hast thou come forth, O pious one?

4. From that perishable and very evil world, thou hast come unto this imperishable, unmolested world.

5. Therefore taste immortality, for here you see pleasure eternally."

6. And after that, Ataro, the angel of the fire of Auharmazd, came forward, saluted me,

7. and said thus: "A fine supplier art thou, Arda Viraf, of green wood, who art the messenger of the Mazdayasnians!"

8. Then I saluted, and said

9. thus: "Thy servant, O Ataro the angel, it was who, in the world, always put upon thee wood and perfume seven years old,

10. and you exclaim about my green wood!"

11. Then Ataro, the angel of the fire of Auharmazd, said

12. thus: "Come on, that I may show thee the tank of water of the green wood which was put upon me."

13. And he led me on to a place, and showed the blue water of a large tank,

14. and said: "This is the water which that wood exuded, which thou puttedst upon me."

CHAPTER XI

1. Afterward, arose Vohuman, the archangel, from a throne made of gold,

2. and he took hold of my hand; with the words "good thought" and "good word" and "good deed," he brought

me into the midst of Auharmazd and the archangels and other holy ones,

3. and the guardian angels of Zaratusht Spitama, Kai-Vishtasp, Jamasp, Isadvastar the son of Zaratusht, and other upholders and leaders of the religion,

4. than whom I have never seen any one more brilliant and excellent.

5. And Vohuman said

6. thus: " This is Auharmazd."

7. And I wished to offer worship before him.

8. And he said to me thus: " Salutation to thee, Arda Viraf, thou art welcome;

9. from that perishable world thou hast come to this pure, bright place."

10. And he ordered Srosh the pious, and Ataro the angel,

11. thus: " Take Arda Viraf, and show him the place and reward of the pious,

12. and also the punishment of the wicked."

13. Then Srosh the pious, and Ataro the angel, took hold of my hand;

14. and I was led by them from place to place.

15. I also saw the archangels, and I beheld the other angels;

16. I also saw the guardian angels of Gayomard, Zaratusht, Kai-Vishtasp, Frashoshtar, Jamasp, and other well-doers and leaders of the religion.

CHAPTER XII

1. I also came to a place, and saw

2. the souls of the liberal, who walked adorned,

3. and were above the other souls, in all splendor;

4. and Auharmazd ever exalts the souls of the liberal, who are brilliant and elevated and mighty.

5. And I said thus: " Happy art thou who art a soul of the liberal, that are thus above the other souls."

6. And it seemed to me sublime.

7. I also saw the souls of those who, in the world, chanted the Gathas and used the prescribed prayers (*yeshts*),

8. and were steadfast in the good religion of the Mazdayasnians, which Auharmazd taught to Zaratusht;

9. when I advanced, they were in gold-embroidered and silver-embroidered clothes, the most embellished of all clothing.

10. And it seemed to me very sublime.

11. I also saw a soul of those who contract next-of-kin marriages, in material-fashioned splendor,

12. when the lofty splendor of its residence ever increased thereby.

13. And it seemed to me sublime.

14. I also saw the souls of good rulers and monarchs,

15. who ever increased their greatness, goodness, power, and triumph thereby,

16. when they walk in splendor, in their golden trousers.

17. And it seemed to me sublime.

18. I also saw the soul of the great and of truthful speakers, who walked in lofty splendor with great glory.

19. And it seemed to me sublime.

CHAPTER XIII

1. I also saw the souls of those women of excellent thoughts, of excellent words, of excellent deeds, and submissive to control, who consider their husbands as lords,

2. in clothing embroidered with gold and silver, and set with jewels.

3. And I asked thus: "Which souls are those?"

4. And Srosh the pious, and Ataro the angel, said

5. thus: "These are the souls of those women who, in the world, have honored water, and honored fire, and honored

earth and trees, cattle and sheep, and all the other good creations of Auharmazd.

6. And they performed the Yazishn and Dron ceremonies, and the praise and services of God;

7. and they performed the rites and praises of the angels of the heavenly existences, and the angels of the earthly existences;

8. and they practised acquiescence and conformity, reverence and obedience to their husbands and lords.

9. and they were without doubts on the religion of the Mazdayasnians.

10. They were diligent in doing of good works,

11. and they have been abstainers from sin."

12. And it seemed to me sublime.

CHAPTER XIV

1. I also saw the souls of performers of the Yazishn ceremony, and of those who know the scriptures by heart, splendid among the lofty and exalted among the great.[1]

2. And it seemed to me sublime.

3. I also saw the souls of those who solemnized the whole ritual of the religion, and performed and directed the worship of God,

4. who were seated above the other souls;

5. and their good works stood as high as heaven.

6. And it seemed to me very sublime.

7. I also saw the souls of warriors, whose walk was in the supremest pleasure and joyfulness, and together with that of kings;

8. and the well-made arms and equipments of those heroes were made of gold, studded with jewels, well-ornamented and all embroidered;

9. and they were in wonderful trousers [2] with much pomp and power and triumph.

10. And it seemed to me sublime.

[1] " Splendid in what is lofty, and exalted in what is great."
[2] " Greaves "; but more probably " coronets and crowns."

11. I also saw the souls of those who killed many noxious creatures (*khrafstras*) in the world;

12. and the prosperity of the waters and sacred fires, and fires in general, and trees, and the prosperity also of the earth was ever increased thereby; and they were exalted and adorned.

13. And it seemed to me very sublime.

14. I also saw the souls of agriculturists, in a splendid place, and glorious and thick majestic clothing;

15. as they stood, and offered praise, before the spirits of water and earth, trees and cattle;

16. and they utter thanksgiving and praise and benediction;

17. their throne also is great, and the place they occupy is good.

18. And it seemed to me sublime.

19. I also saw the souls of artizans who, in the world, served their rulers and chieftains;

20. as they saw on thrones which were well-carpeted and great, splendid and embellished.

21. And it seemed to me very sublime.

CHAPTER XV

1. I also saw the souls of shepherds, by whom, in the world, quadrupeds and sheep were employed and fed,

2. and preserved from the wolf and thief and tyrannical man.

3. And at appointed times, water and grass and food were given;

4. and they were preserved from severe cold and heat; .

5. and the males were allowed access at the usual time, and properly restrained when inopportune;

6. whereby very great advantage, profit and benefit, food and clothing were afforded to the men of that time:

7. Which souls walked among those who are brilliant, on a beautiful eminence, in great pleasure and joy.

8. And it seemed to me very sublime.

9. I also saw many golden thrones, fine carpets and cushions decked with rich cloth,

10. on which are seated the souls of householders and justices, who were heads of village families, and exercised mediation and authority,

11. and made a desolate place prosperous;

12. they also brought many conduits, streams, and fountains for the improvement of tillage and cultivation, and the advantage of creatures.

13. And as they stand before those who are the guardian angels of water, and of trees, and also of the pious, in great power and triumph,

14. they offer them blessings and praise, and repeat thanksgivings.

15. And it seemed to me very sublime.

16. I also saw the souls of the faithful, the teachers and inquirers, in the greatest gladness on the splendid throne.

17. And it seemed to me sublime.

18. I also saw the friendly souls of interceders and peace-seekers,

19. who ever increased thereby their brilliance, which was like the stars and moon and sun;

20. and they ever walked agreeably in the light of the atmosphere.

21. I also saw the pre-eminent world of the pious, which is the all-glorious light of space, much perfumed with sweet basil, all-bedecked, all-admired, and splendid, full of glory and every joy and every pleasure,

22. with which no one is satiated.

CHAPTER XVI

1. Afterward, Srosh the pious, and Ataro the angel, took hold of my hand, and I went thence onward.

2. I came to a place, and I saw a great river which was gloomy as dreadful hell;

3. on which river were many souls and guardian angels;

4. and some of them were not able to cross, and some crossed only with great difficulty, and some crossed easily.

5. And I asked thus: "What river is this? and who are these people who stand so distressed?"

6. Srosh the pious, and Ataro the angel, said

7. thus: "This river is the many tears which men shed from the eyes, as they make lamentation and weeping for the departed.

8. They shed those tears unlawfully, and they swell to this river.

9. Those who are not able to cross over are those for whom, after their departure, much lamentation and weeping were made;

10. and those who cross more easily are those for whom less was made.

11. Speak forth to the world thus: 'When you are in the world, make no lamentation and weeping unlawfully;

12. 'for so much harm and difficulty may happen to the souls of your departed.'"

CHAPTER XVII

1. I came back again to the Chinvat bridge.

2. And I saw a soul of those who were wicked, when in those first three nights so much mischief and evil were shown to their souls, as never such distress was seen by them in the world.

3. And I inquired of Srosh the pious, and Ataro the angel, thus: "Whose soul is this?"

4. Srosh the pious, and Ataro the angel, said

5. thus: "This soul of the wicked wandered there where the wicked one died, over the place where the life went forth;

6. it stood at his head, and uttered the Gatha words

7. thus: 'Creator Auharmazd! to which land do I go? and what do I take as a refuge?'

8. And as much misfortune and difficulty happen to him, that night,

9. as in the world, unto a man who lived in the world and lived in difficulty and misfortune."

10. Afterward, a stinking cold wind comes to meet him.

11. So it seemed to that soul as if it came forth from the northern quarter, from the quarter of the demons,[1] a more stinking wind than which he had not perceived in the world.

12. And in that wind he saw his own religion and deeds as a profligate woman, naked, decayed, gapping, bandy-legged, lean-hipped, and unlimitedly spotted[2] so that spot was joined to spot, like the most hideous, noxious creature, most filthy and most stinking.

13. Then that wicked soul spoke thus: "Who art thou, than whom I never saw any one of the creatures of Auharmazd and Akharman uglier, or filthier, or more stinking?"

14. To him she spoke thus: "I am thy bad actions, O youth of evil thoughts, of evil words, of evil deeds, of evil religion.

15. It is on account of thy will and actions that I am hideous and vile, iniquitous and diseased, rotten and foul-smelling, unfortunate and distressed, as appears to thee.

16. When thou sawest any one who performed the Yazishn and Dron ceremonies, and praise and prayer and the service of God;

17. and preserved and protected water and fire, cattle and trees, and other good creations;

18. thou practisedst the will of Akharman and the demons, and improper actions.

19. And when thou sawest one who provided hospitable

---

[1] The north is supposed to be the special residence of Akharman and the demons, and hell is also referred to the same region.

[2] Or, perhaps, scaled.

reception, and gave something deservedly in gifts and charity, for the advantage of the good and worthy who came from far, and who were from near;

20. thou wast avaricious, and shuttedst up thy door.

21. And though I have been unholy,[3] I am made more unholy through thee;

22. and though I have been frightful, I am made more frightful through thee;

23. though I have been tremulous, I am made more tremulous through thee;

24. though I am settled in the northern region of the demons, I am settled farther north through thee;

25. through these evil thoughts, and through these evil words, and through these evil deeds, which thou practisedst.

26. They curse me, a long time, in the long execration and evil communion of the evil spirit."

27. Afterward, that soul of the wicked advanced the first footstep on Dush-humat [4] and the second footstep on Dush-hukt,[5] and the third on Dushhuvarsht;[6] and with the fourth footstep he ran to hell.

CHAPTER XVIII

1. Afterward, Srosh the pious, and Ataro the angel, took hold of my hand,

2. so that I went on unhurt.

3. In that manner, I beheld cold and heat, drought and stench,

4. to such a degree as I never saw, nor heard of, in the world.

5. And when I went farther,

6. I also saw the greedy jaws of hell, like the most frightful pit, descending in a very narrow and fearful place;

7. in darkness so gloomy that it is necessary to hold by the hand;

[3] That is, I have been considered bad.
[4] The place of evil thoughts.
[5] The place of evil words.
[6] The place of evil deeds.

8. and in such stench that every one whose nose inhales that air will struggle and stagger and fall;

9. and on account of such close confinement no one's existence is possible;

10. and every one thinks thus: "I am alone";

11. and when three days and nights have elapsed he says thus: "The nine thousand years [1] are completed, and they will not release me!"

12. Everywhere, even the lesser noxious creatures (*khrafstras*) are as high as mountains,

13. and they so tear and seize and worry the souls of the wicked, as would be unworthy of a dog.

14. And I easily passed in there, with Srosh the pious, the well-grown and triumphant, and Ataro the angel.

CHAPTER XIX

1. I came to a place, and I saw the soul of a man,

2. through the fundament of which soul, as it were a snake, like a beam, went in, and came forth out of the mouth;

3. and many other snakes ever seized all the limbs.

4. And I inquired of Srosh the pious, and Ataro the angel,

5. thus: "What sin was committed by this body, whose soul suffers so severe a punishment?"

6. Srosh the pious, and Ataro the angel, said

7. thus: "This is the soul of that wicked man, who, in the world, committed sodomy, now the soul suffers so severe a punishment."

[From here onward the pictures of the tortured souls become too nauseous to follow.]

---

[1] At the end of which the opposition of Akharman is to cease and the resurrection to take place.

This is the end of this publication.

Any remaining blank pages are for our book binding
requirements and are blank on purpose.

To search thousands of interesting publications like this one,
please remember to visit our website at:

http://www.kessinger.net

www.ingramcontent.com/pod-product-compliance
Lightning Source LLC
LaVergne TN
LVHW061940060326
832903LV00047B/251